Guide to Flutter

Practical Guide

V. Telman

Copyright © 2024

Guide to Flutter

1.Introduction to Flutter

Flutter is an open-source mobile application development framework created by Google. It allows developers to create high-quality mobile applications for both Android and iOS platforms using a single codebase. Flutter provides a rich set of widgets that enable developers to build beautiful and responsive user interfaces.

One of the key features of Flutter is its hot reload functionality, which allows developers to make changes to their code and see the results instantly on their emulator or physical device. This makes the development process incredibly fast and efficient, as developers can quickly iterate on their designs and fix bugs without having to recompile the entire application.

Flutter also uses a reactive programming model, which allows developers to easily manage the state of their application and update the user interface in response to user interactions or changes in data. This makes it easier to build complex and interactive applications without having to deal with the complexities of traditional app development.

Another benefit of using Flutter is its performance. Flutter apps are compiled directly to native machine code, which means they can run at near-native speeds on both Android and iOS devices. This makes Flutter a great choice for building high-performance applications that require smooth animations and fast response times.

In addition to its performance and productivity benefits, Flutter also has a strong community of developers who contribute to its growth and development. There are plenty of resources available online, including documentation, tutorials, and sample projects, that can help developers learn how to use Flutter and build their own mobile applications.

Overall, Flutter is a powerful and versatile framework that is rapidly gaining popularity among mobile developers. Its ease of use, fast development cycle, and performance make it an excellent choice for building mobile apps that look great and perform well on a variety of devices. Whether you're a beginner looking to get started with mobile app development or an experienced developer looking to streamline your workflow, Flutter is definitely worth considering for your next project.

2. Flutter Installation Guide

In this guide, we will walk you through the process of installing Flutter on your machine. Flutter is a popular open-source framework for building cross-platform apps for iOS and Android. It allows developers to write code once and run it on multiple platforms, saving time and effort.

Before we begin, please make sure you have the following prerequisites installed on your machine:

1. macOS, Windows, or Linux operating system
2. Disk space: 600 MB (doesn't include disk space for IDE/tools).
3. Tools: Flutter depends on these command-line tools being available in your environment.
   * Windows PowerShell 5.0 or newer (this is pre-installed with Windows 10)
   * Git for Windows 2.x, with the Use Git from the Windows Command Prompt option.

Now let's get started with the installation process:

Step 1: Download Flutter
To download Flutter, visit the official Flutter website at flutter.dev. Click on the "Get Started" button and then select your operating system (macOS, Windows, or Linux). Follow the instructions to download the Flutter SDK.

Step 2: Extract the Flutter SDK
Once the download is complete, unzip the Flutter SDK archive to a location on your machine. For example, on macOS or Linux, you can extract it to your home directory. On Windows, you can extract it to C:\src\flutter.

Step 3: Add Flutter to your PATH
To be able to run Flutter commands from the terminal, you need to add the Flutter binary path to your PATH environment variable. For macOS and Linux, you can do this by adding the following line to your ~/.bashrc or ~/.zshrc file:

```bash
export PATH="$PATH:`pwd`/flutter/bin"
```

For Windows, you can do this by adding the Flutter binary path to your PATH system variable. To do this, open the System Properties dialog, go to the "Advanced" tab, and click on the "Environment Variables" button. In the "System variables" section, find the "Path" variable, click on "Edit", and add the Flutter binary path (e.g., C:\src\flutter\bin) to the list of paths.

Step 4: Verify the Flutter installation
To verify that Flutter has been successfully installed, open a new terminal window and run the following command:

```bash
flutter doctor
```

This command will check your Flutter installation and provide information about any missing dependencies that need to be installed. Follow the instructions provided to install any missing dependencies.

Step 5: Install an IDE (Optional)
While you can use any text editor to write

Flutter code, it is recommended to use an Integrated Development Environment (IDE) for a better coding experience. The two most popular IDEs for Flutter development are Visual Studio Code and Android Studio.

To install Visual Studio Code, visit code.visualstudio.com and download the appropriate version for your operating system. Once installed, you can install the Flutter and Dart extensions from the Visual Studio Code marketplace.

To install Android Studio, visit developer.android.com/studio and download the Android Studio IDE. Make sure to install the Flutter and Dart plugins from the Android Studio plugin marketplace.

Step 6: Create a new Flutter project
Once you have set up your development environment, you can create a new Flutter project by running the following command in the terminal:

```bash
flutter create my_flutter_app
```

```

Replace "my_flutter_app" with the name of your project. This command will create a new Flutter project with the default project structure.

Step 7: Run your Flutter app
To run your Flutter app on an emulator or physical device, navigate to the root directory of your project and run the following command:

```bash
flutter run
```

This command will build your Flutter app and launch it on the emulator or device. You can make changes to your code and see the changes reflected in real-time by saving the file and hot reloading the app.

Congratulations! You have successfully installed Flutter on your machine and created your first Flutter project. You are now ready to start building cross-platform apps with
```

Flutter.

Flutter is a powerful framework for building cross-platform apps that run on both iOS and Android devices. Its ease of use, hot reload feature, and rich set of widgets make it a popular choice among developers. By following this installation guide, you can set up Flutter on your machine and start building apps in no time.

3. Setting Up the Development Environment

Prerequisites

Before you start developing with Flutter, you need to have a few tools and software installed on your machine. These prerequisites include:

- **Operating System**: Flutter works on Windows, macOS, and Linux.
- **Flutter SDK**: This is the software development kit that includes everything you need to develop Flutter applications.
- **IDE**: Flutter supports various Integrated Development Environments (IDEs) like Android Studio, IntelliJ IDEA, and Visual Studio Code.
- **Android Studio**: This is needed for Android development. Even if you plan to develop for iOS, having Android Studio installed can be beneficial as it includes Android SDK, which Flutter uses.
- **Xcode**: Required for iOS development, only available on macOS.
- **Web Browser**: Needed for developing and testing web applications.

Creating a Flutter Project

Using the Command Line

1. Open a terminal.
2. Run the following command to create a new Flutter project:

    ```sh
    flutter create hello_flutter
    ```

3. Navigate into the project directory:

    ```sh
    cd hello_flutter
    ```

4. Open the project in your preferred IDE.

Using Android Studio

1. Open Android Studio.
2. Select `Start a new Flutter project`.
3. Choose `Flutter Application` and click

`Next`.
4. Enter your project name (e.g., `hello_flutter`), and choose the Flutter SDK path.
5. Click `Finish` to create the project.

Project Structure

A typical Flutter project structure looks like this:

```
hello_flutter/
  android/
  build/
  ios/
  lib/
    main.dart
  test/
  .gitignore
  .metadata
  pubspec.yaml
  README.md
```

- **lib/**: Contains Dart code.
- **main.dart**: Entry point of the

application.
- **pubspec.yaml**: Configuration file for managing dependencies and assets.

main.dart, Hot Reload, and Flutter Inspector

main.dart

The `main.dart` file is the entry point of a Flutter application. Here's a basic example:

```dart
import 'package:flutter/material.dart';

void main() {
  runApp(MyApp());
}

class MyApp extends StatelessWidget {
  @override
  Widget build(BuildContext context) {
    return MaterialApp(
      title: 'Hello Flutter',
      home: Scaffold(
        appBar: AppBar(
          title: Text('Hello Flutter'),
```

```
    ),
    body: Center(
      child: Text('Welcome to Flutter!'),
    ),
   ),
  );
 }
}
```

Hot Reload

Hot Reload allows you to instantly see the result of your code changes without restarting the app. To use Hot Reload:

1. Make changes in your Dart code.
2. Save the file.
3. The changes will automatically be reflected in the running app.

Hot Reload works by injecting updated source code files into the running Dart Virtual Machine (VM). This only affects the state of the app, meaning the state is preserved during Hot Reload.

Flutter Inspector

The Flutter Inspector is a tool for visualizing and exploring the widget tree of your Flutter application. It helps you understand how your UI is structured and how widgets are related to each other.

To use the Flutter Inspector in Android Studio:

1. Run your app in debug mode.
2. Open the Flutter Inspector tab.
3. Use the Inspector to explore the widget tree.

Basics of Dart

Introduction to Dart

Dart is a client-optimized programming language for developing fast apps on any platform. It is the language used to develop Flutter applications. Here are some key features of Dart:

- **Compiled Language**: Dart can be compiled to ARM and x64 machine code, as

well as JavaScript.
- **Strongly Typed**: Dart is a statically typed language, meaning that the type of a variable is known at compile time.
- **Object-Oriented**: Everything in Dart is an object, and Dart supports concepts like inheritance, mixins, and interfaces.

Basic Syntax

Variables

Variables in Dart can be declared using the `var`, `final`, or `const` keywords.

```dart
var name = 'Flutter';
final age = 3;
const pi = 3.14;
```

- `var`: Can be reassigned.
- `final`: Can be set only once.
- `const`: Compile-time constant.

Functions

Functions in Dart are defined using the `void` keyword for functions that don't return a value, or the type of the value they return.

```dart
void main() {
  print('Hello, Dart!');
}

int add(int a, int b) {
  return a + b;
}
```

Classes

Dart is object-oriented, and classes are used to create objects.

```dart
class Person {
  String name;
  int age;

  Person(this.name, this.age);

  void introduce() {
```

```
    print('Hello, my name is $name and I am $age years old.');
  }
}

void main() {
  var person = Person('Alice', 30);
  person.introduce();
}
```

The Framework: Technical Details

Widgets

Flutter is built around the concept of widgets. Widgets are the basic building blocks of a Flutter app's user interface. Each widget is an immutable declaration of part of the user interface.

There are two types of widgets in Flutter:

- **Stateful Widgets**: Widgets that can change their state during the lifetime of the app.
- **Stateless Widgets**: Widgets that cannot

change their state once they are built.

Rendering

Flutter's rendering engine is responsible for rendering the widgets to the screen. It uses Skia, an open-source 2D graphics library, to draw the UI. The rendering process involves several steps:

1. **Build Phase**: Flutter creates a widget tree by calling the build methods of widgets.
2. **Layout Phase**: Flutter calculates the position and size of each widget.
3. **Painting Phase**: Flutter draws the widgets on the screen.

State Management

Managing state is a crucial aspect of Flutter development. There are several approaches to state management in Flutter:

- **setState()**: The simplest way to manage state in a StatefulWidget.
- **InheritedWidget**: Used to pass data down the widget tree.

- **Provider**: A popular state management package.
- **Riverpod**: An improvement over Provider.
- **Bloc/Cubit**: Business Logic Component pattern for managing state.

Stateful and Stateless Widgets

Stateless Widget

A Stateless Widget is immutable, meaning its properties cannot change once the widget is built. Here's an example of a Stateless Widget:

```dart
import 'package:flutter/material.dart';

class MyStatelessWidget extends StatelessWidget {
  @override
  Widget build(BuildContext context) {
    return Scaffold(
      appBar: AppBar(
        title: Text('Stateless Widget'),
      ),
```

```dart
    body: Center(
      child: Text('I am a stateless widget'),
    ),
   );
  }
 }
```

Stateful Widget

A Stateful Widget, on the other hand, is mutable. It can change its state during the lifetime of the widget. Here's an example of a Stateful Widget:

```dart
import 'package:flutter/material.dart';

class MyStatefulWidget extends StatefulWidget {


  @override
  _MyStatefulWidgetState createState() => _MyStatefulWidgetState();
}
```

```dart
class _MyStatefulWidgetState extends State<MyStatefulWidget> {
  int _counter = 0;

  void _incrementCounter() {
    setState(() {
      _counter++;
    });
  }

  @override
  Widget build(BuildContext context) {
    return Scaffold(
      appBar: AppBar(
        title: Text('Stateful Widget'),
      ),
      body: Center(
        child: Column(
          mainAxisAlignment: MainAxisAlignment.center,
          children: <Widget>[
            Text('You have pushed the button this many times:'),
            Text('$_counter', style: Theme.of(context).textTheme.headline4),
          ],
        ),
```

```
    ),
    floatingActionButton: FloatingActionButton(
      onPressed: _incrementCounter,
      tooltip: 'Increment',
      child: Icon(Icons.add),
    ),
  );
 }
}
```

StatefulWidget Lifecycle

A StatefulWidget has a lifecycle that includes the following stages:

1. **createState()**: Called when the widget is created.
2. **initState()**: Called once when the state object is created.
3. **didChangeDependencies()**: Called when the dependencies change.
4. **build()**: Called to build the widget.
5. **setState()**: Called to update the state.
6. **deactivate()**: Called when the widget is removed from the tree.

7. **dispose()**: Called when the state object is removed.

Understanding these stages helps in managing resources and handling state changes efficiently.

Example: Combining Stateful and Stateless Widgets

Here's an example of how you might combine Stateful and Stateless Widgets in a Flutter app:

```dart
import 'package:flutter/material.dart';

void main() {
  runApp(MyApp());
}

class MyApp extends StatelessWidget {
  @override
  Widget build(BuildContext context) {
    return MaterialApp(
      title: 'Flutter Demo',
      home: MyHomePage(),
```

```dart
      );
    }
}

class MyHomePage extends StatefulWidget {
  @override
  _MyHomePageState createState() =>
_MyHomePageState();
}

class _MyHomePageState extends
State<MyHomePage> {
  String _displayText = 'Hello, Flutter!';

  void _updateText() {
    setState(() {
      _displayText = 'You pressed the button!';
    });
  }

  @override
  Widget build(BuildContext context) {
    return Scaffold(
      appBar: AppBar(
        title: Text('Flutter Demo'),
      ),
      body: Center(
```

```dart
      child: Column(
        mainAxisAlignment:
MainAxisAlignment.center,
        children: <Widget>[
          MyStatelessWidget(displayText:
_displayText),
          ElevatedButton(
            onPressed: _updateText,
            child: Text('Press Me'),
          ),
        ],
      ),
    ),
  );
 }
}

class MyStatelessWidget extends StatelessWidget {
  final String displayText;

  MyStatelessWidget({required this.displayText});

  @override
  Widget build(BuildContext context) {
    return Text(displayText);
```

```
    }
  }
```

In this example, `MyHomePage` is a StatefulWidget that manages the state of the `_displayText` string. The `MyStatelessWidget` displays the text, and the `ElevatedButton` updates the state when pressed.

Conclusion

Setting up the development environment for Flutter involves installing the necessary tools and software, including the Flutter SDK, an IDE, and any platform-specific tools required for Android and iOS development. Creating a Flutter project is straightforward, and you can use either the command line or an IDE like Android Studio or Visual Studio Code.

The `main.dart` file serves as the entry point for your application, and tools like Hot Reload and Flutter Inspector make the development process more efficient and enjoyable. Understanding the basics of Dart is crucial, as it is the language used to develop Flutter applications.

The Flutter framework is built around widgets, which are the fundamental building blocks of the user interface. Widgets can be either stateful or stateless, depending on whether they need to manage state changes.

By combining Stateful and Stateless Widgets, you can create complex and dynamic user interfaces. Understanding the lifecycle of a StatefulWidget helps in managing resources and handling state changes efficiently.

With this knowledge, you are well-equipped to start building Flutter applications and exploring the rich features and capabilities of the Flutter framework.

4. Flutter Development: Comprehensive Guide

Managing Images from the Internet

Flutter provides robust capabilities to manage and display images from the internet, enhancing the UI with dynamic content. Using the `Image.network` widget, you can easily load images from a URL.

Basic Example

Here is a basic example of how to use `Image.network`:

```dart
import 'package:flutter/material.dart';

void main() {
  runApp(MyApp());
}

class MyApp extends StatelessWidget {
  @override
  Widget build(BuildContext context) {
    return MaterialApp(
```

```dart
      home: Scaffold(
        appBar: AppBar(
          title: Text('Load Image from Internet'),
        ),
        body: Center(
          child: Image.network('https://example.com/image.jpg'),
        ),
      ),
    );
  }
}
```

Handling Errors and Placeholders

You can handle errors and display placeholders while the image is loading using the `CachedNetworkImage` package:

```dart
import 'package:flutter/material.dart';
import 'package:cached_network_image/cached_network_image.dart';
```

```dart
void main() {
  runApp(MyApp());
}

class MyApp extends StatelessWidget {
  @override
  Widget build(BuildContext context) {
    return MaterialApp(
      home: Scaffold(
        appBar: AppBar(
          title: Text('Load Image from Internet with Placeholder'),
        ),
        body: Center(
          child: CachedNetworkImage(
            imageUrl: 'https://example.com/image.jpg',
            placeholder: (context, url) => CircularProgressIndicator(),
            errorWidget: (context, url, error) => Icon(Icons.error),
          ),
        ),
      ),
    );
  }
}
```

```

### Container Widget: Single-Child Layout

The `Container` widget in Flutter is versatile and used for single-child layouts. It can be styled with properties such as padding, margin, alignment, and decoration.

#### Basic Usage

```dart
import 'package:flutter/material.dart';

void main() {
  runApp(MyApp());
}

class MyApp extends StatelessWidget {
  @override
  Widget build(BuildContext context) {
    return MaterialApp(
      home: Scaffold(
        appBar: AppBar(
          title: Text('Container Example'),
        ),
        body: Center(

```
      child: Container(
        width: 200,
        height: 100,
        color: Colors.blue,
        child: Center(
          child: Text(
            'Hello, Container!',
            style: TextStyle(color: Colors.white),
          ),
        ),
      ),
    ),
  );
 }
}
```

Properties

- **alignment**: Aligns the child within the container.
- **padding**: Adds padding inside the container.
- **margin**: Adds margin outside the container.

- **decoration**: Adds decorations such as background color, border, and shadows.
- **width and height**: Sets the dimensions of the container.

Managing Assets and Images

Flutter allows you to manage and use assets such as images, fonts, and more in your application. This is done through the `pubspec.yaml` file.

Adding Images to the Project

1. Create an `assets` directory in the root of your Flutter project.
2. Add your image files to this directory.
3. Reference these assets in the `pubspec.yaml` file:

```yaml
flutter:
  assets:
    - assets/image1.png
    - assets/image2.jpg
```

Using Asset Images

To use an asset image in your Flutter app, use the `Image.asset` widget:

```dart
import 'package:flutter/material.dart';

void main() {
  runApp(MyApp());
}

class MyApp extends StatelessWidget {
  @override
  Widget build(BuildContext context) {
    return MaterialApp(
      home: Scaffold(
        appBar: AppBar(
          title: Text('Asset Image Example'),
        ),
        body: Center(
          child: Image.asset('assets/image1.png'),
        ),
      ),
    );
  }
}
```

```

### Text Widget and Text Styles

The `Text` widget in Flutter is used to display a string of text with single or multiple styles.

#### Basic Usage

```dart
import 'package:flutter/material.dart';

void main() {
 runApp(MyApp());
}

class MyApp extends StatelessWidget {
 @override
 Widget build(BuildContext context) {
  return MaterialApp(
   home: Scaffold(
    appBar: AppBar(
     title: Text('Text Widget Example'),
    ),
    body: Center(
     child: Text('Hello, Flutter!'),
    ),

```
      ),
    );
  }
}
```

Styling Text

You can style text using the `TextStyle` class:

```dart
import 'package:flutter/material.dart';

void main() {
  runApp(MyApp());
}

class MyApp extends StatelessWidget {
  @override
  Widget build(BuildContext context) {
    return MaterialApp(
      home: Scaffold(
        appBar: AppBar(
          title: Text('Text Widget with Style'),
        ),
        body: Center(
          child: Text(
```

```
        'Hello, Flutter!',
        style: TextStyle(
          fontSize: 24,
          fontWeight: FontWeight.bold,
          color: Colors.blue,
        ),
      ),
     ),
    ),
   );
  }
}
```

Button Management with RaisedButton Widget

The `RaisedButton` widget (now deprecated in favor of `ElevatedButton`) is used to create a button with an elevated look.

Basic Usage

```dart
import 'package:flutter/material.dart';

void main() {
```

```
  runApp(MyApp());
}

class MyApp extends StatelessWidget {
 @override
 Widget build(BuildContext context) {
  return MaterialApp(
   home: Scaffold(
    appBar: AppBar(
     title: Text('RaisedButton Example'),
    ),
    body: Center(
     child: RaisedButton(
      onPressed: () {
       print('Button Pressed!');
      },
      child: Text('Press Me'),
     ),
    ),
   ),
  );
 }
}
```

ElevatedButton

With the introduction of Flutter 2.0, it is recommended to use `ElevatedButton`:

```dart
import 'package:flutter/material.dart';

void main() {
  runApp(MyApp());
}

class MyApp extends StatelessWidget {
  @override
  Widget build(BuildContext context) {
    return MaterialApp(
      home: Scaffold(
        appBar: AppBar(
          title: Text('ElevatedButton Example'),
        ),
        body: Center(
          child: ElevatedButton(
            onPressed: () {
              print('Button Pressed!');
            },
            child: Text('Press Me'),
          ),
        ),
      ),
```

      );
    }
}
```

### Row and Column Widgets: Foundations of Multi-Child Layout

The `Row` and `Column` widgets are the primary widgets used for creating multi-child layouts in Flutter. `Row` arranges its children horizontally, and `Column` arranges its children vertically.

#### Row Widget

The `Row` widget places its children in a horizontal array. Here's an example:

```dart
import 'package:flutter/material.dart';

void main() {
  runApp(MyApp());
}

class MyApp extends StatelessWidget {

```dart
@override
Widget build(BuildContext context) {
  return MaterialApp(
    home: Scaffold(
      appBar: AppBar(
        title: Text('Row Widget Example'),
      ),
      body: Center(
        child: Row(
          mainAxisAlignment: MainAxisAlignment.center,
          children: <Widget>[
            Icon(Icons.star, color: Colors.red, size: 50),
            Icon(Icons.star, color: Colors.green, size: 50),
            Icon(Icons.star, color: Colors.blue, size: 50),
          ],
        ),
      ),
    ),
  );
}
}
```

Column Widget

The `Column` widget places its children in a vertical array. Here's an example:

```dart
import 'package:flutter/material.dart';

void main() {
  runApp(MyApp());
}

class MyApp extends StatelessWidget {
  @override
  Widget build(BuildContext context) {
    return MaterialApp(
      home: Scaffold(
        appBar: AppBar(
          title: Text('Column Widget Example'),
        ),
        body: Center(
          child: Column(
            mainAxisAlignment: MainAxisAlignment.center,
            children: <Widget>[
              Icon(Icons.star, color: Colors.red, size: 50),
```

```
        Icon(Icons.star, color: Colors.green, size: 50),
        Icon(Icons.star, color: Colors.blue, size: 50),
      ],
    ),
   ),
  ),
 );
 }
}
```

MainAxisAlignment and CrossAxisAlignment

Both `Row` and `Column` have properties like `mainAxisAlignment` and `crossAxisAlignment` that control how their children are aligned.

- **mainAxisAlignment**: Aligns children along the main axis (horizontal for `Row`, vertical for `Column`).
- **crossAxisAlignment**: Aligns children along the cross axis (vertical for `Row`, horizontal for `Column`).

Example using `mainAxisAlignment` and `crossAxisAlignment`:

```dart
import 'package:flutter/material.dart';

void main() {
  runApp(MyApp());
}

class MyApp extends StatelessWidget {
  @override
  Widget build(BuildContext context) {
    return MaterialApp(
      home: Scaffold(
        appBar: AppBar(
          title: Text('Alignment Example'),
        ),
        body: Center(
          child: Column(
            mainAxisAlignment: MainAxisAlignment.center,
            crossAxisAlignment: CrossAxisAlignment.start,
            children: <Widget>[
              Icon(Icons.star, color: Colors.red,
```

```
              size: 50),
          Icon(Icons.star, color: Colors.green, size: 50),
          Icon(Icons.star, color: Colors.blue, size: 50),
        ],
      ),
    ),
   ),
  );
 }
}
```

Combining Widgets for Complex Layouts

By combining `Container`, `Row`, `Column`, and other widgets, you can create complex and responsive layouts. Here's an example of a more complex layout combining several widgets:

```dart
import 'package:flutter/material.dart';
```

```dart
void main() {
  runApp(MyApp());
}

class MyApp extends StatelessWidget {
  @override
  Widget build(BuildContext context) {
    return MaterialApp(
      home: Scaffold(
        appBar: AppBar(
          title: Text('Complex Layout Example'),
        ),
        body: Padding(
          padding: EdgeInsets.all(16.0),
          child: Column(
            children: <Widget>[
              Container(
                width: double.infinity,
                height: 100,
                color: Colors.blue,
                child: Center(
                  child: Text(
                    'Header',
                    style: TextStyle(color: Colors.white, fontSize: 24),
                  ),
                ),
```

```dart
      ),
      SizedBox(height: 20),
      Row(
        mainAxisAlignment:
MainAxisAlignment.spaceBetween,
        children: <Widget>[
          Container(
            width: 100,
            height: 100,
            color: Colors.red,
            child: Center(
              child: Text(
                'Left',
                style: TextStyle(color:
Colors.white, fontSize: 18),
              ),
            ),
          ),
          Container(
            width: 100,
            height: 100,
            color: Colors.green,
            child: Center(
              child: Text(
                'Right',
                style: TextStyle(color:
Colors.white, fontSize: 18),
```

```
                  ),
                ),
              ),
            ],
          ),
          SizedBox(height: 20),
          Container(
            width: double.infinity,
            height: 100,
            color: Colors.orange,
            child: Center(
              child: Text(
                'Footer',
                style: TextStyle(color: Colors.white, fontSize: 24),
              ),
            ),
          ),
        ],
      ),
    ),
  ),
 );
 }
}
```

Flutter provides a comprehensive set of widgets and tools to create dynamic, visually appealing, and responsive user interfaces. By mastering the use of widgets like `Container`, `Row`, `Column`, `Text`, and `ElevatedButton`, you can build complex layouts and manage assets and images efficiently. Understanding these foundational elements of Flutter will enable you to create engaging and user-friendly applications.

5. Fundamentals of Dart (in Flutter)

Dart is a client-optimized language for fast apps on any platform. It is the language used to develop Flutter applications. Understanding Dart's fundamentals is crucial for building efficient and effective Flutter apps. This guide will cover the basics of Dart, including variables, functions, and classes.

Introduction to Dart

Dart is an object-oriented, class-based, garbage-collected language with C-style syntax. It was developed by Google and is used to build mobile, desktop, server, and web applications. Dart compiles to native machine code as well as JavaScript, making it versatile for various platforms.

Variables

Variables in Dart can hold data and are defined using the `var`, `final`, or `const` keywords.

Using `var`

The `var` keyword is used when the type of the variable can be inferred from the assigned value.

```dart
void main() {
  var name = 'John';
  print(name); // Output: John
}
```

Using `final`

The `final` keyword is used for variables that should only be assigned once. Once a `final` variable is set, it cannot be changed.

```dart
void main() {
  final age = 25;
  // age = 26; // This will cause an error
  print(age); // Output: 25
}
```

Using `const`

The `const` keyword is used for compile-time constants. `const` variables must be assigned a value that can be determined at compile time.

```dart
void main() {
  const pi = 3.14;
  // pi = 3.1415; // This will cause an error
  print(pi); // Output: 3.14
}
```

Functions

Functions in Dart are used to encapsulate a sequence of statements that can be executed repeatedly.

Basic Function

A simple function that prints a message:

```dart
void greet() {
  print('Hello, Dart!');
```

```dart
}

void main() {
  greet(); // Output: Hello, Dart!
}
```

Function with Parameters

Functions can accept parameters to make them more flexible.

```dart
void greet(String name) {
  print('Hello, $name!');
}

void main() {
  greet('Alice'); // Output: Hello, Alice!
}
```

Function with Return Value

Functions can also return a value.

```dart
```

```dart
int add(int a, int b) {
  return a + b;
}

void main() {
  int sum = add(3, 4);
  print(sum); // Output: 7
}
```

Arrow Functions

For concise functions, Dart provides arrow syntax.

```dart
int add(int a, int b) => a + b;

void main() {
  int sum = add(3, 4);
  print(sum); // Output: 7
}
```

Classes and Objects

Dart is an object-oriented language, and

everything in Dart is an object, including numbers, functions, and `null`. Classes are the blueprint for creating objects.

Defining a Class

A class can be defined using the `class` keyword.

```dart
class Person {
  String name;
  int age;

  Person(this.name, this.age);

  void introduce() {
    print('Hello, my name is $name and I am $age years old.');
  }
}
```

Creating Objects

You can create an instance of a class (an object) using the `new` keyword or directly.

```dart
void main() {
  var person1 = Person('Alice', 30);
  Person person2 = Person('Bob', 25);

  person1.introduce(); // Output: Hello, my name is Alice and I am 30 years old.
  person2.introduce(); // Output: Hello, my name is Bob and I am 25 years old.
}
```

Named Constructors

Classes can have named constructors for more control over object creation.

```dart
class Person {
  String name;
  int age;

  Person(this.name, this.age);

  Person.withName(this.name) : age = 0;
```

```dart
  void introduce() {
    print('Hello, my name is $name and I am $age years old.');
  }
}

void main() {
  var person = Person.withName('Charlie');
  person.introduce(); // Output: Hello, my name is Charlie and I am 0 years old.
}
```

Inheritance

Dart supports inheritance, which allows you to create a new class that is based on an existing class.

```dart
class Person {
  String name;
  int age;

  Person(this.name, this.age);

  void introduce() {
```

```dart
    print('Hello, my name is $name and I am $age years old.');
  }
}

class Student extends Person {
  String school;

  Student(String name, int age, this.school) : super(name, age);

  @override
  void introduce() {
    print('Hello, my name is $name, I am $age years old, and I study at $school.');
  }
}

void main() {
  var student = Student('Dave', 20, 'XYZ University');
  student.introduce(); // Output: Hello, my name is Dave, I am 20 years old, and I study at XYZ University.
}
```

Getters and Setters

You can define getters and setters to access and modify private properties of a class.

```dart
class Rectangle {
  double _width;
  double _height;

  Rectangle(this._width, this._height);

  double get width => _width;
  set width(double value) => _width = value;

  double get height => _height;
  set height(double value) => _height = value;

  double get area => _width * _height;
}

void main() {
  var rect = Rectangle(5, 10);
  print('Area: ${rect.area}'); // Output: Area: 50

  rect.width = 7;
```

```
  print('Updated Area: ${rect.area}'); //
Output: Updated Area: 70
}
```

Dart is a powerful language with features that make it suitable for building fast and efficient applications. Understanding the fundamentals of Dart, including variables, functions, and classes, is essential for any developer working with Flutter. By mastering these concepts, you can build robust and maintainable Flutter applications.

6. Advanced Flutter: Building Complex UI and Managing State

In this comprehensive guide, we will explore advanced Flutter concepts, including the use of `Stack` widget for overlaying widgets, `ListView` for list management, creating tabs and drawers for navigation, handling floating action buttons and snack bars, managing dialogs, and using `ThemeData` for consistent theming. We will also delve into creating and using stateful widgets with practical examples.

Stack Widget for Overlaying Widgets

The `Stack` widget allows you to overlay multiple widgets on top of each other. It is useful for scenarios where you need to position widgets relative to each other in a non-linear fashion, such as adding a floating button on top of an image or text over a background.

Basic Usage

```dart
```

```dart
import 'package:flutter/material.dart';

void main() {
  runApp(MyApp());
}

class MyApp extends StatelessWidget {
  @override
  Widget build(BuildContext context) {
    return MaterialApp(
      home: Scaffold(
        appBar: AppBar(title: Text('Stack Example')),
        body: Stack(
          children: <Widget>[
            Container(
              width: 300,
              height: 300,
              color: Colors.red,
            ),
            Positioned(
              top: 50,
              left: 50,
              child: Container(
                width: 100,
                height: 100,
                color: Colors.blue,
```

```
          ),
        ),
        Positioned(
          bottom: 20,
          right: 20,
          child: Container(
            width: 50,
            height: 50,
            color: Colors.green,
          ),
        ),
      ],
    ),
   ),
  );
 }
}
```

In this example, the `Stack` widget contains three containers. The `Positioned` widget is used to place the second and third containers at specific positions within the stack.

ListView: The Widget for Managing Lists

`ListView` is a scrolling widget that helps you

create scrollable lists of widgets. It's highly versatile and can be used for both static and dynamic content.

Basic Usage

```dart
import 'package:flutter/material.dart';

void main() {
  runApp(MyApp());
}

class MyApp extends StatelessWidget {
  @override
  Widget build(BuildContext context) {
    return MaterialApp(
      home: Scaffold(
        appBar: AppBar(title: Text('ListView Example')),
        body: ListView(
          children: <Widget>[
            ListTile(
              leading: Icon(Icons.map),
              title: Text('Map'),
            ),
            ListTile(
```

```
          leading: Icon(Icons.photo_album),
          title: Text('Album'),
        ),
        ListTile(
          leading: Icon(Icons.phone),
          title: Text('Phone'),
        ),
      ],
    ),
   ),
  );
 }
}
```

In this example, `ListView` contains a list of `ListTile` widgets, which display icons and text.

Creating Tabs

Tabs allow you to organize content into multiple panels that users can switch between. Flutter provides `TabBar` and `TabBarView` widgets to create tabs.

Basic Usage

```dart
import 'package:flutter/material.dart';

void main() {
  runApp(MyApp());
}

class MyApp extends StatelessWidget {
  @override
  Widget build(BuildContext context) {
    return MaterialApp(
      home: DefaultTabController(
        length: 3,
        child: Scaffold(
          appBar: AppBar(
            title: Text('Tabs Example'),
            bottom: TabBar(
              tabs: [
                Tab(icon: Icon(Icons.directions_car)),
                Tab(icon: Icon(Icons.directions_transit)),
                Tab(icon: Icon(Icons.directions_bike)),
              ],
            ),
```

```
      ),
      body: TabBarView(
        children: [
          Icon(Icons.directions_car),
          Icon(Icons.directions_transit),
          Icon(Icons.directions_bike),
        ],
      ),
    ),
   ),
  );
 }
}
```

In this example, `DefaultTabController` manages the state of the tabs. `TabBar` displays the tabs, and `TabBarView` displays the corresponding content.

Drawer for Accessing Multiple Screens

A drawer provides a sliding panel from the edge of the screen, typically containing navigation links. It's commonly used for app navigation.

Basic Usage

```dart
import 'package:flutter/material.dart';

void main() {
  runApp(MyApp());
}

class MyApp extends StatelessWidget {
  @override
  Widget build(BuildContext context) {
    return MaterialApp(
      home: Scaffold(
        appBar: AppBar(title: Text('Drawer Example')),
        drawer: Drawer(
          child: ListView(
            padding: EdgeInsets.zero,
            children: <Widget>[
              DrawerHeader(
                child: Text('Header'),
                decoration: BoxDecoration(
                  color: Colors.blue,
                ),
              ),
              ListTile(
```

```
        title: Text('Item 1'),
        onTap: () {
          // Handle the item tap
        },
      ),
      ListTile(
        title: Text('Item 2'),
        onTap: () {
          // Handle the item tap
        },
      ),
     ],
    ),
   ),
   body: Center(
     child: Text('Swipe from the left edge to see the drawer.'),
     ),
    ),
   );
  }
}
```

In this example, a `Drawer` widget is added to the `Scaffold`. It contains a header and a list of items. Swiping from the left edge of the screen will reveal the drawer.

Creating a Floating Action Button and Snack Bar

A Floating Action Button (FAB) is a circular button that floats above the content. A Snack Bar is a lightweight message that briefly appears at the bottom of the screen.

Basic Usage

```dart
import 'package:flutter/material.dart';

void main() {
  runApp(MyApp());
}

class MyApp extends StatelessWidget {
  @override
  Widget build(BuildContext context) {
    return MaterialApp(
      home: Scaffold(
        appBar: AppBar(title: Text('FAB and Snack Bar Example')),
        body: Center(
```

```
        child: Text('Press the button to show a Snack Bar.'),
      ),
      floatingActionButton: FloatingActionButton(
        onPressed: () {
          ScaffoldMessenger.of(context).showSnackBar(
            SnackBar(
              content: Text('Hello! This is a Snack Bar.'),
            ),
          );
        },
        tooltip: 'Show Snack Bar',
        child: Icon(Icons.add),
      ),
    ),
  );
 }
}
```
```

In this example, pressing the FAB shows a Snack Bar with a message.
```

Managing Dialogs

Dialogs are used to alert users, confirm actions, or display additional information.

Basic Usage

```dart
import 'package:flutter/material.dart';

void main() {
  runApp(MyApp());
}

class MyApp extends StatelessWidget {
  @override
  Widget build(BuildContext context) {
    return MaterialApp(
      home: Scaffold(
        appBar: AppBar(title: Text('Dialog Example')),
        body: Center(
          child: ElevatedButton(
            onPressed: () {
              showDialog(
                context: context,
                builder: (BuildContext context) {
```

```
        return AlertDialog(
          title: Text('Alert'),
          content: Text('This is a simple alert dialog.'),
          actions: <Widget>[
            TextButton(
              child: Text('Close'),
              onPressed: () {
                Navigator.of(context).pop();
              },
            ),
          ],
        );
      },
    );
  },
  child: Text('Show Dialog'),
),
     ),
    ),
   );
  }
}
```

In this example, pressing the button shows an alert dialog with a title, content, and a close button.

ThemeData for Sharing Styles via Themes

`ThemeData` allows you to define and share a consistent look and feel throughout your app. You can customize colors, fonts, and other styling elements.

Using ThemeData: Practical Examples

```dart
import 'package:flutter/material.dart';

void main() {
  runApp(MyApp());
}

class MyApp extends StatelessWidget {
  @override
  Widget build(BuildContext context) {
    return MaterialApp(
      title: 'Theme Example',
      theme: ThemeData(
        primarySwatch: Colors.blue,
        textTheme: TextTheme(
```

```
      headline1: TextStyle(fontSize: 72.0, fontWeight: FontWeight.bold),
      bodyText1: TextStyle(fontSize: 14.0, fontFamily: 'Hind'),
    ),
   ),
   home: Scaffold(
    appBar: AppBar(title: Text('Theme Example')),
    body: Center(
     child: Column(
      mainAxisAlignment: MainAxisAlignment.center,
      children: <Widget>[
       Text('This is headline1 style', style: Theme.of(context).textTheme.headline1),
       Text('This is bodyText1 style', style: Theme.of(context).textTheme.bodyText1),
      ],
     ),
    ),
   ),
  );
 }
}
```

In this example, `ThemeData` is used to define a primary color and text styles for the app. The styles are then applied to the `Text` widgets using `Theme.of(context).textTheme`.

Creating a Stateful Widget

Stateful widgets maintain state that can change during the lifetime of the widget. This is useful for interactive elements that need to update dynamically.

Practical Example of Creating a Stateful Widget

```dart
import 'package:flutter/material.dart';

void main() {
  runApp(MyApp());
}

class MyApp extends StatelessWidget {
  @override
  Widget build(BuildContext context) {
    return MaterialApp(
      title: 'Stateful Widget Example',
```

```
    home: Scaffold(
      appBar: AppBar(title: Text('Stateful Widget Example')),
      body: Center(
        child: CounterWidget(),
      ),
    ),



  );
 }
}

class CounterWidget extends StatefulWidget {
 @override
 _CounterWidgetState createState() => _CounterWidgetState();
}

class _CounterWidgetState extends State<CounterWidget> {
 int _counter = 0;

 void _incrementCounter() {
  setState(() {
   _counter++;
  });
```

```
  }

  @override
  Widget build(BuildContext context) {
    return Column(
      mainAxisAlignment: MainAxisAlignment.center,
      children: <Widget>[
        Text(
          'You have pushed the button this many times:',
        ),
        Text(
          '$_counter',
          style: Theme.of(context).textTheme.headline4,
        ),
        ElevatedButton(
          onPressed: _incrementCounter,
          child: Text('Increment Counter'),
        ),
      ],
    );
  }
}
```

In this example, `CounterWidget` is a stateful widget with a `_counter` state. The `_incrementCounter` method updates the state, and the UI reflects the new state using `setState`.

Flutter provides a powerful toolkit for building complex and interactive UIs. By mastering widgets like `Stack`, `ListView`, tabs, drawers, FABs, snack bars, and dialogs, you can create dynamic and user-friendly applications. Additionally, using `ThemeData` allows for consistent theming across your app, and understanding state management with stateful widgets is crucial for building responsive applications. With these tools and concepts, you are well-equipped to develop advanced Flutter applications that provide a rich user experience.

7. Creating a Flutter Application

Flutter is an open-source UI software development toolkit created by Google. It is used to develop cross-platform applications for Android, iOS, Linux, macOS, Windows, Google Fuchsia, and the web from a single codebase. In this guide, we'll go through the steps to create a Flutter application, understand the project structure, explore layouts and widgets, and manage state.

Creating a Flutter Project

To create a new Flutter project, you need to have Flutter installed on your machine. If you haven't done that yet, you can follow the [installation guide] (https://flutter.dev/docs/get-started/install) on the official Flutter website.

Using the Command Line

1. Open a terminal.
2. Run the following command to create a new Flutter project:

```sh
flutter create my_app
```

3. Navigate into the project directory:

```sh
cd my_app
```

4. Open the project in your preferred IDE. For example, using Visual Studio Code, you can run:

```sh
code .
```

Using Android Studio

1. Open Android Studio.
2. Select `Start a new Flutter project`.
3. Choose `Flutter Application` and click `Next`.
4. Enter your project name (e.g., `my_app`), and choose the Flutter SDK path.

5. Click `Finish` to create the project.

Project Structure

A typical Flutter project has the following structure:

```
my_app/
  android/
  build/
  ios/
  lib/
    main.dart
  test/
  .gitignore
  .metadata
  pubspec.yaml
  README.md
```

- **android/**: Contains the Android-specific code and configurations.
- **ios/**: Contains the iOS-specific code and configurations.
- **lib/**: Contains the Dart code for your application. The `main.dart` file is the entry

point of the application.
- **test/**: Contains the unit and widget tests.
- **pubspec.yaml**: A configuration file that manages the dependencies and assets for your project.

Layout and Widgets

Flutter's UI is built using widgets, which are the building blocks of a Flutter application. Widgets describe what their view should look like given their current configuration and state.

Basic Layout Example

Here's an example of a basic Flutter application with a simple layout:

```dart
import 'package:flutter/material.dart';

void main() {
  runApp(MyApp());
}

class MyApp extends StatelessWidget {
```

```
@override
Widget build(BuildContext context) {
  return MaterialApp(
    title: 'Flutter Demo',
    home: Scaffold(
      appBar: AppBar(
        title: Text('Flutter Demo Home Page'),
      ),
      body: Center(
        child: Column(
          mainAxisAlignment: MainAxisAlignment.center,
          children: <Widget>[
            Text('Hello, Flutter!'),
            SizedBox(height: 20),
            ElevatedButton(
              onPressed: () {},
              child: Text('Press Me'),
            ),
          ],
        ),
      ),
    ),
  );
}
}
```

In this example, `MyApp` is a stateless widget that builds the main structure of the app. It uses `MaterialApp` to set up the application, and `Scaffold` to provide a default app bar, body, and other components. The body of the `Scaffold` contains a `Center` widget, which centers its child within itself. The child is a `Column` widget that arranges its children vertically.

Managing State

State management is an essential aspect of building Flutter applications. It determines how the UI should be updated in response to state changes. Flutter provides several ways to manage state, including `StatefulWidget`, `InheritedWidget`, and external packages like `Provider` and `Riverpod`.

StatefulWidget

A `StatefulWidget` is a widget that has mutable state. When the state changes, the widget rebuilds.

Example of StatefulWidget

```dart
import 'package:flutter/material.dart';

void main() {
 runApp(MyApp());
}

class MyApp extends StatelessWidget {
 @override
 Widget build(BuildContext context) {
  return MaterialApp(
    title: 'StatefulWidget Demo',
    home: CounterWidget(),
  );
 }
}

class CounterWidget extends StatefulWidget {
 @override
 _CounterWidgetState createState() =>
_CounterWidgetState();
}

class _CounterWidgetState extends State<CounterWidget> {
```

```dart
int _counter = 0;

void _incrementCounter() {
  setState(() {
    _counter++;
  });
}

@override
Widget build(BuildContext context) {
  return Scaffold(
    appBar: AppBar(
      title: Text('StatefulWidget Demo'),
    ),
    body: Center(
      child: Column(
        mainAxisAlignment:
MainAxisAlignment.center,
        children: <Widget>[
          Text('You have pushed the button this many times:'),
          Text(
            '$_counter',
            style:
Theme.of(context).textTheme.headline4,
          ),
        ],
```

```
      ),
    ),
    floatingActionButton: FloatingActionButton(
      onPressed: _incrementCounter,
      tooltip: 'Increment',
      child: Icon(Icons.add),
    ),
  );
 }
}
```

In this example, `CounterWidget` is a `StatefulWidget` that displays a counter. The `_incrementCounter` method increments the counter and calls `setState`, which tells Flutter to rebuild the widget with the new state.

Provider for State Management

`Provider` is a third-party package that simplifies state management. It allows you to inject and access state objects in your widget tree efficiently.

Example using Provider

1. Add `provider` to your `pubspec.yaml`:

```yaml
dependencies:
  flutter:
    sdk: flutter
  provider: ^6.0.0
```

2. Create a `Counter` class that extends `ChangeNotifier`:

```dart
import 'package:flutter/foundation.dart';

class Counter with ChangeNotifier {
  int _count = 0;

  int get count => _count;

  void increment() {
    _count++;
    notifyListeners();
  }
}
```

3. Use `ChangeNotifierProvider` to provide the `Counter` class to the widget tree:

```dart
import 'package:flutter/material.dart';
import 'package:provider/provider.dart';

void main() {
  runApp(
    ChangeNotifierProvider(
      create: (context) => Counter(),
      child: MyApp(),
    ),
  );
}

class MyApp extends StatelessWidget {
  @override
  Widget build(BuildContext context) {
    return MaterialApp(
      title: 'Provider Demo',
      home: CounterWidget(),
    );
  }
}
```

```dart
class CounterWidget extends StatelessWidget {
  @override
  Widget build(BuildContext context) {
    return Scaffold(
      appBar: AppBar(
        title: Text('Provider Demo'),
      ),
      body: Center(
        child: Column(
          mainAxisAlignment: MainAxisAlignment.center,
          children: <Widget>[
            Text('You have pushed the button this many times:'),
            Consumer<Counter>(
              builder: (context, counter, child) {
                return Text(
                  '${counter.count}',
                  style: Theme.of(context).textTheme.headline4,
                );
              },
            ),
          ],
        ),
      ),
```

```
      floatingActionButton:
FloatingActionButton(
        onPressed: () =>
context.read<Counter>().increment(),
        tooltip: 'Increment',
        child: Icon(Icons.add),
      ),
    );
  }
}
```

In this example, the `Counter` class manages the state and notifies listeners when the state changes. The `ChangeNotifierProvider` widget provides the `Counter` instance to the widget tree. The `Consumer` widget listens for changes and rebuilds when the state changes.

Creating a Flutter application involves setting up a new project, understanding the project structure, building layouts with widgets, and managing state. By mastering these fundamental concepts, you can develop powerful and responsive Flutter applications that run on multiple platforms. Whether you choose to manage state with `StatefulWidget` or external packages like `Provider`, Flutter provides the flexibility and tools needed to build high-quality applications.

8. Advanced Flutter Development: Data Passing, Routing, and State Management

In this guide, we will delve into more advanced concepts of Flutter development. We will cover how to pass data between screens, manage routes, handle data, use APIs to retrieve data, save and retrieve data locally, and manage application state. Each section includes detailed explanations and practical examples.

Passing Data Between Screens

Passing data between screens in Flutter is essential for building dynamic applications where user interactions on one screen influence the content displayed on another. There are several methods to pass data between screens in Flutter.

Using the Navigator

The `Navigator` widget manages a stack of route objects and provides methods for navigating between them.

Example: Passing Data with Navigator.push

```dart
import 'package:flutter/material.dart';

void main() {
  runApp(MyApp());
}

class MyApp extends StatelessWidget {
  @override
  Widget build(BuildContext context) {
    return MaterialApp(
      title: 'Data Passing Example',
      home: FirstScreen(),
    );
  }
}

class FirstScreen extends StatelessWidget {
  @override
  Widget build(BuildContext context) {
    return Scaffold(
      appBar: AppBar(title: Text('First Screen')),
```

```dart
      body: Center(
        child: ElevatedButton(
          onPressed: () {
            Navigator.push(
              context,
              MaterialPageRoute(
                builder: (context) =>
  SecondScreen(data: 'Hello from First Screen'),
              ),
            );
          },
          child: Text('Go to Second Screen'),
        ),
      ),
    );
  }
}

class SecondScreen extends StatelessWidget {
  final String data;

  SecondScreen({required this.data});

  @override
  Widget build(BuildContext context) {
    return Scaffold(
      appBar: AppBar(title: Text('Second
```

```
      Screen')),
        body: Center(
          child: Text(data),
        ),
      );
    }
  }
```

In this example, the `FirstScreen` passes a string to the `SecondScreen` using `Navigator.push` and `MaterialPageRoute`.

Using Named Routes

Named routes allow you to navigate using route names and pass arguments.

Example: Passing Data with Named Routes

```dart
import 'package:flutter/material.dart';

void main() {
  runApp(MyApp());
}
```

```dart
class MyApp extends StatelessWidget {
  @override
  Widget build(BuildContext context) {
    return MaterialApp(
      title: 'Named Routes Example',
      initialRoute: '/',
      routes: {
        '/': (context) => FirstScreen(),
        '/second': (context) => SecondScreen(),
      },
      onGenerateRoute: (settings) {
        if (settings.name == '/second') {
          final args = settings.arguments as ScreenArguments;
          return MaterialPageRoute(
            builder: (context) {
              return SecondScreen(
                title: args.title,
                message: args.message,
              );
            },
          );
        }
        assert(false, 'Need to implement ${settings.name}');
        return null;
```

```dart
      },
    );
  }
}

class ScreenArguments {
  final String title;
  final String message;

  ScreenArguments(this.title, this.message);
}

class FirstScreen extends StatelessWidget {
  @override
  Widget build(BuildContext context) {
    return Scaffold(
      appBar: AppBar(title: Text('First Screen')),
      body: Center(
        child: ElevatedButton(
          onPressed: () {
            Navigator.pushNamed(
              context,
              '/second',
              arguments: ScreenArguments(
                'Second Screen',
                'Hello from First Screen',
```

```dart
          ),
        );
      },
      child: Text('Go to Second Screen'),
    ),
   ),
  );
 }
}

class SecondScreen extends StatelessWidget {
 final String title;
 final String message;

 SecondScreen({required this.title, required this.message});

 @override
 Widget build(BuildContext context) {
  return Scaffold(
   appBar: AppBar(title: Text(title)),
   body: Center(
    child: Text(message),
   ),
  );
 }
}
```

```

In this example, `ScreenArguments` class is used to pass multiple pieces of data to the `SecondScreen` using named routes.

## Managing Routes

Routing is the process of navigating between different screens or pages within an application. Flutter provides robust routing mechanisms to manage the navigation stack and pass data efficiently.

### Setting Up Routes

#### Example: Basic Route Management

```dart
import 'package:flutter/material.dart';

void main() {
  runApp(MyApp());
}

class MyApp extends StatelessWidget {
  @override

```dart
Widget build(BuildContext context) {
  return MaterialApp(
    title: 'Route Management Example',
    initialRoute: '/',
    routes: {
      '/': (context) => HomeScreen(),
      '/second': (context) => SecondScreen(),
    },
  );
 }
}

class HomeScreen extends StatelessWidget {
 @override
 Widget build(BuildContext context) {
   return Scaffold(
     appBar: AppBar(title: Text('Home Screen')),
     body: Center(
       child: ElevatedButton(
         onPressed: () {
           Navigator.pushNamed(context, '/second');
         },
         child: Text('Go to Second Screen'),
       ),
     ),
```

```dart
      );
    }
  }

  class SecondScreen extends StatelessWidget {
    @override
    Widget build(BuildContext context) {
      return Scaffold(
        appBar: AppBar(title: Text('Second Screen')),
        body: Center(
          child: ElevatedButton(
            onPressed: () {
              Navigator.pop(context);
            },
            child: Text('Back to Home Screen'),
          ),
        ),
      );
    }
  }
```

In this example, the `initialRoute` is set to the home screen, and the routes are defined in the `routes` map.

Using onGenerateRoute

The `onGenerateRoute` callback allows you to define more complex routing logic.

Example: Using onGenerateRoute

```dart
import 'package:flutter/material.dart';

void main() {
  runApp(MyApp());
}

class MyApp extends StatelessWidget {
  @override
  Widget build(BuildContext context) {
    return MaterialApp(
      title: 'onGenerateRoute Example',
      initialRoute: '/',
      onGenerateRoute: (settings) {
        switch (settings.name) {
          case '/':
            return MaterialPageRoute(builder: (context) => HomeScreen());
          case '/second':
            final args = settings.arguments as
```

```
String;
        return MaterialPageRoute(
          builder: (context) => SecondScreen(data: args),
        );
      default:
        return MaterialPageRoute(builder: (context) => UnknownScreen());
    }
  },
);
 }
}

class HomeScreen extends StatelessWidget {
 @override
 Widget build(BuildContext context) {
  return Scaffold(
    appBar: AppBar(title: Text('Home Screen')),
    body: Center(
      child: ElevatedButton(
        onPressed: () {
         Navigator.pushNamed(context, '/second', arguments: 'Hello from Home Screen');
        },
```

```dart
          child: Text('Go to Second Screen'),
        ),
      ),
    );
  }
}

class SecondScreen extends StatelessWidget {
  final String data;

  SecondScreen({required this.data});

  @override
  Widget build(BuildContext context) {
    return Scaffold(
      appBar: AppBar(title: Text('Second Screen')),
      body: Center(
        child: Text(data),
      ),
    );
  }
}

class UnknownScreen extends StatelessWidget {
  @override
```

```
  Widget build(BuildContext context) {
    return Scaffold(
      appBar: AppBar(title: Text('Unknown Screen')),
      body: Center(
        child: Text('Unknown route'),
      ),
    );
  }
}
```

In this example, `onGenerateRoute` is used to handle routing, including passing arguments and handling unknown routes.

Data Management

Managing data effectively is crucial for building robust Flutter applications. This involves retrieving, storing, and updating data.

Using Provider for State Management

The `Provider` package is widely used for state management in Flutter.

Example: Using Provider

1. Add `provider` to your `pubspec.yaml`:

```yaml
dependencies:
  flutter:
    sdk: flutter
  provider: ^6.0.0
```

2. Create a `Counter` class:

```dart
import 'package:flutter/foundation.dart';

class Counter with ChangeNotifier {
  int _count = 0;

  int get count => _count;

  void increment() {
    _count++;
    notifyListeners();
  }
}
```

3. Use `ChangeNotifierProvider` and `Consumer`:

```dart
import 'package:flutter/material.dart';
import 'package:provider/provider.dart';

void main() {
  runApp(
    ChangeNotifierProvider(
      create: (context) => Counter(),
      child: MyApp(),
    ),
  );
}

class MyApp extends StatelessWidget {
  @override
  Widget build(BuildContext context) {
    return MaterialApp(
      title: 'Provider Example',
      home: CounterScreen(),
    );
  }
}
```

```dart
class CounterScreen extends StatelessWidget {
  @override
  Widget build(BuildContext context) {
    return Scaffold(
      appBar: AppBar(title: Text('Provider Example')),
      body: Center(
        child: Column(
          mainAxisAlignment: MainAxisAlignment.center,
          children: <Widget>[
            Text('You have pushed the button this many times:'),
            Consumer<Counter>(
              builder: (context, counter, child) {
                return Text(
                  '${counter.count}',
                  style: Theme.of(context).textTheme.headline4,
                );
              },
            ),
          ],
        ),
      ),
      floatingActionButton:
```

```
      FloatingActionButton(
        onPressed: () => context.read<Counter>().increment(),
        tooltip: 'Increment',
        child: Icon(Icons.add),
      ),
    );
  }
}
```

In this example, `Provider` is used to manage and share the state of the `Counter` class across the widget tree.

Using APIs to Retrieve Data

Flutter can interact with RESTful APIs to retrieve and display data.

Example: Fetching Data from an API

1. Add `http` to your `pubspec.yaml`:

   ```yaml
   ```

```
dependencies:
  flutter:
    sdk: flutter
  http: ^0.13.3
```

2. Create a function to fetch data:

```dart
import 'dart:convert';
import 'package:flutter/material.dart';
import 'package:http/http.dart' as http;

void main() {
  runApp(MyApp());
}

class MyApp extends StatelessWidget {
  @override
  Widget build(BuildContext context) {
    return MaterialApp(
      title: 'API Example',
      home: ApiScreen(),
    );
  }
}
```

```dart
class ApiScreen extends StatefulWidget {
  @override
  _ApiScreenState createState() => _ApiScreenState();
}

class _ApiScreenState extends State<ApiScreen> {
  Future<List<Post>> fetchPosts() async {
    final response = await http.get(Uri.parse('https://jsonplaceholder.typicode.com/posts'));

    if (response.statusCode == 200) {
      List jsonResponse = json.decode(response.body);
      return jsonResponse.map((post) => Post.fromJson(post)).toList();
    } else {
      throw Exception('Failed to load posts');
    }
  }

  @override
  Widget build(BuildContext context) {
    return Scaffold(
      appBar: AppBar(title: Text('API
```

```
Example')),
    body: FutureBuilder<List<Post>>(
      future: fetchPosts(),
      builder: (context, snapshot) {
        if (snapshot.connectionState ==
ConnectionState.waiting) {
          return Center(child:
CircularProgressIndicator());
        } else if (snapshot.hasError) {
          return Center(child: Text('Error: $
{snapshot.error}'));
        } else if (!snapshot.hasData ||
snapshot.data!.isEmpty) {
          return Center(child: Text('No data
found'));
        } else {
          return ListView.builder(
            itemCount: snapshot.data!.length,
            itemBuilder: (context, index) {
              return ListTile(
                title: Text(snapshot.data!
[index].title),
                subtitle: Text(snapshot.data!
[index].body),
              );
            },
          );
```

```dart
          }
        },
      ),
    );
  }
}

class Post {
  final int userId;
  final int id;
  final String title;
  final String body;

  Post({
    required this.userId,
    required this.id,
    required this.title,
    required this.body,
  });

  factory Post.fromJson(Map<String, dynamic> json) {
    return Post(
      userId: json['userId'],
      id: json['id'],
      title: json['title'],
      body: json['body'],
```

```
      );
    }
  }
```

In this example, data is fetched from a REST API and displayed in a `ListView` using `FutureBuilder`.

Saving and Retrieving Data Locally

Local storage is essential for persisting data across app sessions. Flutter supports various local storage solutions, including `SharedPreferences` and SQLite.

Using SharedPreferences

`SharedPreferences` is a simple key-value store for storing small amounts of data.

Example: Using SharedPreferences

1. Add `shared_preferences` to your `pubspec.yaml`:

   ```yaml
   ```

```yaml
dependencies:
  flutter:
    sdk: flutter
  shared_preferences: ^2.0.6
```

2. Save and retrieve data:

```dart
import 'package:flutter/material.dart';
import 'package:shared_preferences/shared_preferences.dart';

void main() {
  runApp(MyApp());
}

class MyApp extends StatelessWidget {
  @override
  Widget build(BuildContext context) {
    return MaterialApp(
      title: 'SharedPreferences Example',
      home: SharedPreferencesScreen(),
    );
  }
}
```

```dart
class SharedPreferencesScreen extends StatefulWidget {
  @override
  _SharedPreferencesScreenState createState() =>
      _SharedPreferencesScreenState();
}

class _SharedPreferencesScreenState extends State<SharedPreferencesScreen> {
  int _counter = 0;

  @override
  void initState() {
    super.initState();
    _loadCounter();
  }

  // Load counter value from SharedPreferences
  void _loadCounter() async {
    final prefs = await SharedPreferences.getInstance();
    setState(() {
      _counter = prefs.getInt('counter') ?? 0;
    });
```

```dart
  }

  // Increment counter and save it to SharedPreferences
  void _incrementCounter() async {
    final prefs = await SharedPreferences.getInstance();
    setState(() {
      _counter++;
      prefs.setInt('counter', _counter);
    });
  }

  @override
  Widget build(BuildContext context) {
    return Scaffold(
      appBar: AppBar(title: Text('SharedPreferences Example')),
      body: Center(
        child: Column(
          mainAxisAlignment: MainAxisAlignment.center,
          children: <Widget>[
            Text('You have pushed the button this many times:'),
            Text(
              '$_counter',
```

```
          style:
Theme.of(context).textTheme.headline4,
        ),
      ],
    ),
  ),
    floatingActionButton:
FloatingActionButton(
      onPressed: _incrementCounter,
      tooltip: 'Increment',
      child: Icon(Icons.add),
    ),
  );
 }
}
```

In this example, the counter value is saved to and retrieved from `SharedPreferences`.

Managing Application State

State management is crucial for creating responsive and dynamic applications. Flutter offers several state management solutions, including `Provider`, `Bloc`, `Riverpod`, and `StateNotifier`.

Using Provider for State Management

`Provider` is a popular state management solution in Flutter.

Example: Using Provider

1. Add `provider` to your `pubspec.yaml`:

    ```yaml
    dependencies:
      flutter:
        sdk: flutter
      provider: ^6.0.0
    ```

2. Create a `Counter` class:

    ```dart
    import 'package:flutter/foundation.dart';

    class Counter with ChangeNotifier {
      int _count = 0;

      int get count => _count;
    ```

```
  void increment() {
    _count++;
    notifyListeners();
  }
}
```

3. Use `ChangeNotifierProvider` and `Consumer`:

```dart
import 'package:flutter/material.dart';
import 'package:provider/provider.dart';

void main() {
  runApp(
    ChangeNotifierProvider(
      create: (context) => Counter(),
      child: MyApp(),
    ),
  );
}

class MyApp extends StatelessWidget {
  @override
  Widget build(BuildContext context) {
    return MaterialApp(
```

```dart
      title: 'Provider Example',
      home: CounterScreen(),
    );
  }
}


class CounterScreen extends StatelessWidget {
  @override
  Widget build(BuildContext context) {
    return Scaffold(
      appBar: AppBar(title: Text('Provider Example')),
      body: Center(
        child: Column(
          mainAxisAlignment: MainAxisAlignment.center,
          children: <Widget>[
            Text('You have pushed the button this many times:'),
            Consumer<Counter>(
              builder: (context, counter, child) {
                return Text(
                  '${counter.count}',
                  style: Theme.of(context).textTheme.headline4,
                );
```

```
      },
    ),
   ],
  ),
 ),
 floatingActionButton: FloatingActionButton(
    onPressed: () => context.read<Counter>().increment(),
    tooltip: 'Increment',
    child: Icon(Icons.add),
  ),
 );
 }
}
```

In this example, `Provider` is used to manage and share the state of the `Counter` class across the widget tree.

Using Bloc for State Management

`Bloc` is another popular state management library that implements the BLoC (Business Logic Component) pattern.

Example: Using Bloc

1. Add `flutter_bloc` and `equatable` to your `pubspec.yaml`:

   ```yaml
   dependencies:
     flutter:
       sdk: flutter
     flutter_bloc: ^8.0.0
     equatable: ^2.0.3
   ```

2. Create a `CounterCubit`:

   ```dart
   import 'package:bloc/bloc.dart';
   import 'package:equatable/equatable.dart';

   class CounterCubit extends Cubit<int> {
     CounterCubit() : super(0);

     void increment() => emit(state + 1);
   }
   ```

3. Use `BlocProvider` and `BlocBuilder`:

```dart
import 'package:flutter/material.dart';
import 'package:flutter_bloc/flutter_bloc.dart';

void main() {
  runApp(MyApp());
}

class MyApp extends StatelessWidget {
  @override
  Widget build(BuildContext context) {
    return MaterialApp(
      title: 'Bloc Example',
      home: BlocProvider(
        create: (context) => CounterCubit(),
        child: CounterScreen(),
      ),
    );
  }
}

class CounterScreen extends StatelessWidget {
  @override
  Widget build(BuildContext context) {
```

```dart
    return Scaffold(
      appBar: AppBar(title: Text('Bloc Example')),
      body: Center(
        child: Column(
          mainAxisAlignment: MainAxisAlignment.center,
          children: <Widget>[
            Text('You have pushed the button this many times:'),
            BlocBuilder<CounterCubit, int>(
              builder: (context, count) {
                return Text(
                  '$count',
                  style: Theme.of(context).textTheme.headline4,
                );
              },
            ),
          ],
        ),
      ),
      floatingActionButton: FloatingActionButton(
        onPressed: () => context.read<CounterCubit>().increment(),
```

```
      tooltip: 'Increment',
      child: Icon(Icons.add),
    ),
  );
 }
}
```

In this example, `Bloc` is used to manage and share the state of the `CounterCubit` across the widget tree.

In this comprehensive guide, we covered advanced Flutter concepts, including passing data between screens, managing routes, handling data, using APIs, saving and retrieving data locally, and managing application state. By mastering these concepts, you can build robust, dynamic, and responsive Flutter applications that provide a seamless user experience. Whether you use `Provider`, `Bloc`, or other state management solutions, Flutter offers the flexibility and tools needed to develop high-quality applications.

9. Navigating Between Screens in a Flutter App

Introduction

In Flutter, navigation refers to moving between different screens or "routes" within an application. Effective navigation is crucial for providing a smooth user experience and ensuring that users can easily access different parts of the app. Flutter provides a powerful navigation and routing system that allows developers to manage screens efficiently and pass data between them seamlessly.

Navigation and Routing: The Basics

Navigation in Flutter is primarily managed through the `Navigator` class. This class manages a stack of `Route` objects and provides methods to push and pop routes onto and off of the stack. Each route typically corresponds to a screen or a page in your application.

Routes

In Flutter, a route is an abstraction for a "screen" or a "page" in your app. Each route is represented by a `PageRoute` object. When you navigate to a new screen, you push a new route onto the navigator's stack. Conversely, when you navigate back, you pop the current route off the stack.

Navigator

The `Navigator` class manages the routes for your application. It maintains a stack of routes and provides methods to manipulate the stack, such as `push`, `pop`, `pushNamed`, `popAndPushNamed`, etc. The navigator is typically accessed using `Navigator.of(context)`.

MaterialApp and Navigator

In a typical Flutter application, the root widget is usually a `MaterialApp`. This widget sets up important features like the navigation stack (`Navigator`) and provides easy access to common Material Design widgets and styles.

Navigator and Named Routes: Practical

Examples

Setting Up Named Routes

Named routes provide a way to identify routes using a simple string rather than directly creating and pushing `PageRoute` objects. This approach makes your codebase more readable and easier to maintain.

```dart
void main() => runApp(MyApp());

class MyApp extends StatelessWidget {
 @override
 Widget build(BuildContext context) {
  return MaterialApp(
    initialRoute: '/', // default route
    routes: {
     '/': (context) => HomeScreen(),
     '/details': (context) => DetailsScreen(),
    },
  );
 }
}
```

In this example, `HomeScreen` is set as the initial route, and `DetailsScreen` is registered with the route name '/details'. Now, you can navigate to `DetailsScreen` using `Navigator.pushNamed(context, '/details')`.

Practical Navigation Examples

Pushing a New Screen

```dart
Navigator.push(
  context,
  MaterialPageRoute(builder: (context) => DetailsScreen()),
);
```

Popping Back to the Previous Screen

```dart
Navigator.pop(context);
```

Pushing Named Routes

```dart
```

```dart
Navigator.pushNamed(context, '/details');
```

Popping Until a Specific Route

```dart
Navigator.popUntil(context, ModalRoute.withName('/home'));
```

Managing Navigation State

Navigation and State Management

As your app grows, managing navigation state becomes crucial. Here are a few tips for effectively managing navigation in Flutter:

- **Use Named Routes**: Helps in maintaining a clear structure and makes it easier to navigate between screens without hardcoding navigation logic.

- **State Management**: Consider using state management solutions like Provider, Bloc, or Riverpod to manage state across different screens and maintain data integrity.

- **Nested Navigation**: For complex UI flows, consider using nested navigators with `Navigator` and `NavigatorState` to manage different parts of your app independently.

Passing Data to a Route

In Flutter, you can pass data to a route when navigating to it. This can be achieved by passing arguments to the `Navigator` when pushing a new route.

```dart
Navigator.push(
  context,
  MaterialPageRoute(
    builder: (context) => DetailsScreen(data: 'Hello from Home'),
  ),
);
```

In the `DetailsScreen`, you can then access this data:

```dart
```

```dart
class DetailsScreen extends StatelessWidget {
  final String data;

  DetailsScreen({required this.data});

  @override
  Widget build(BuildContext context) {
    return Scaffold(
      appBar: AppBar(title: Text('Details')),
      body: Center(
        child: Text(data),
      ),
    );
  }
}
```

Exchanging Data Between Named Routes

To exchange data between named routes, you can use `onGenerateRoute` in your `MaterialApp`. This allows you to handle data passing and route generation dynamically.

```dart
MaterialApp(
  onGenerateRoute: (settings) {
```

```dart
    if (settings.name == '/details') {
      final args = settings.arguments as Map<String, dynamic>;
      return MaterialPageRoute(
        builder: (context) => DetailsScreen(data: args['data']),
      );
    }
  },
);
```

When navigating to `/details`, you can pass data like this:

```dart
Navigator.pushNamed(
  context,
  '/details',
  arguments: {'data': 'Hello from Home'},
);
```

In `DetailsScreen`, you can access the passed data similarly as shown in the previous example.

Navigation in Flutter is fundamental to building rich, interactive applications. By understanding the basics of navigation and routing, leveraging named routes, and effectively managing navigation state, you can create intuitive user experiences and maintain a clean and scalable codebase. Flutter's navigation system provides powerful tools to navigate between screens, pass data efficiently, and handle complex UI flows. As you continue to develop Flutter applications, mastering these navigation techniques will be essential for building successful apps.

10. Project Organization in Flutter

Introduction

Organizing your Flutter project effectively is crucial for maintaining clarity, scalability, and maintainability as your application grows. A well-organized project structure not only improves collaboration among team members but also enhances code reuse and facilitates debugging and testing processes. In this guide, we will explore best practices and strategies for organizing a Flutter project.

Flutter Project Structure

Default Project Structure

When you create a new Flutter project using `flutter create`, Flutter generates a default project structure. This structure includes:

- **lib/**: This directory contains your Dart code.
- **android/** and **ios/**: These directories contain platform-specific configuration files and code for Android and iOS respectively.

- **assets/**: This directory can contain files like images, fonts, etc., which are bundled with your app.
- **test/**: This directory is for unit tests.

Recommended Project Structure

While the default structure is a good starting point, as your project grows, you might want to organize it further for better management. Here's a recommended project structure:

- **lib/**
  - **screens/**: Contains all screen/widget definitions.
  - **models/**: Data models used throughout the app.
  - **services/**: Services such as API clients, database helpers, etc.
  - **utils/**: Utility functions and helpers.
  - **widgets/**: Reusable UI components.
  - **themes/**: Theme configurations for the app.
  - **routes.dart**: Centralized route definitions using named routes.
- **assets/**: For static files like images, fonts, etc.

- **test/**: Unit tests.
- **android/** and **ios/**: Platform-specific configurations.

Key Principles of Organization

1. **Modularity**: Divide your app into smaller modules or layers (e.g., UI, data, business logic) to keep related functionalities together and separate concerns.

2. **Naming Conventions**: Use meaningful names for directories, files, classes, and variables to make your codebase more understandable.

3. **Centralization**: Centralize configurations, routes, and constants to minimize duplication and make global changes easier.

4. **Separation of Concerns**: Keep UI-related code separate from business logic and data management.

5. **Consistency**: Follow consistent patterns and conventions across your project

to reduce cognitive load for developers.

Storage on Device

Introduction

Flutter provides several options for storing data on the device, depending on the type of data and use case. The main storage options include:

- **File System**: For reading and writing files.
- **Shared Preferences**: For simple key-value pairs.
- **SQLite**: For local relational database storage.

Let's explore each of these storage options in detail.

File System: Reading and Writing Text Files

Reading Files

To read from a text file in Flutter, you can use

the `dart:io` library. Here's an example:

```dart
import 'dart:io';

Future<String> readFile(String filePath) async {
  try {
    File file = File(filePath);
    String content = await file.readAsString();
    return content;
  } catch (e) {
    print("Failed to read file: $e");
    return '';
  }
}
```

Writing Files

To write to a text file:

```dart
import 'dart:io';

Future<void> writeFile(String filePath, String content) async {
```

```dart
  try {
    File file = File(filePath);
    await file.writeAsString(content);
  } catch (e) {
    print("Failed to write file: $e");
  }
}
```

File Operations Best Practices

- Always handle exceptions when reading or writing files.
- Ensure proper file permissions are set, especially on Android.

Shared Preferences

Introduction

Shared Preferences in Flutter allows you to store simple data types (int, double, bool, String) persistently across app sessions. It's typically used for storing user preferences or app settings.

Usage Example

```dart
import 'package:shared_preferences/shared_preferences.dart';

Future<void> savePreference(String key, String value) async {
  SharedPreferences prefs = await SharedPreferences.getInstance();
  prefs.setString(key, value);
}

Future<String?> getPreference(String key) async {
  SharedPreferences prefs = await SharedPreferences.getInstance();
  return prefs.getString(key);
}
```

Best Practices

- Use Shared Preferences for lightweight data only (e.g., user settings).
- Avoid storing large amounts of data or sensitive information.

SQFlite: Managing SQLite Databases with Flutter

Introduction

SQFlite is a Flutter plugin for SQLite databases. It provides a way to store app data in a structured relational database locally on the device. This is useful for storing complex data structures or large amounts of data.

Usage Example

First, add `sqflite` and `path_provider` dependencies to your `pubspec.yaml`.

```yaml
dependencies:
  flutter:
    sdk: flutter
  sqflite: ^2.0.0
  path_provider: ^2.0.2
```

Then, initialize and use SQFlite in your Flutter app:

```dart
import 'package:sqflite/sqflite.dart';
import 'package:path/path.dart' as path;

Future<Database> openDatabase() async {
  String dbPath = await getDatabasesPath();
  String pathToDatabase = path.join(dbPath, 'my_database.db');

  return openDatabase(pathToDatabase, version: 1, onCreate: (db, version) async {
    await db.execute('CREATE TABLE users (id INTEGER PRIMARY KEY, name TEXT)');
  });
}

Future<void> insertUser(String name) async {
  Database db = await openDatabase();
  await db.insert('users', {'name': name});
}

Future<List<Map<String, dynamic>>> getUsers() async {
  Database db = await openDatabase();
  return db.query('users');
```

```
}
```

Best Practices

- Ensure proper error handling and transactions to maintain data integrity.
- Use database migrations (`onUpgrade`) when updating your database schema.

Geolocation and Maps

Geolocation

Geolocation in Flutter allows you to retrieve the current location of the device. This is useful for location-based services such as maps, weather apps, and more.

Using the `geolocator` Package

To use geolocation in Flutter, add the `geolocator` package to your `pubspec.yaml`:

```yaml
dependencies:
  flutter:
```

```
  sdk: flutter
  geolocator: ^7.0.3
```

Example of retrieving the current location:

```dart
import 'package:geolocator/geolocator.dart';

Future<Position?> getCurrentLocation() async {
  bool serviceEnabled;
  LocationPermission permission;

  serviceEnabled = await Geolocator.isLocationServiceEnabled();
  if (!serviceEnabled) {
    return Future.error('Location services are disabled.');
  }

  permission = await Geolocator.checkPermission();
  if (permission == LocationPermission.denied) {
    permission = await Geolocator.requestPermission();
```

```
  if (permission ==
LocationPermission.denied) {
    return Future.error('Location permissions
are denied.');
   }
 }

  if (permission ==
LocationPermission.deniedForever) {
    return Future.error(
      'Location permissions are permanently
denied, we cannot request permissions.');
  }

  return await
Geolocator.getCurrentPosition();
}
```

Best Practices

- Handle location permissions properly.
- Provide meaningful error messages when location services or permissions are not available.

Managing Maps

Introduction

Integrating maps into your Flutter app allows you to display geographic data visually and interactively. Google Maps is a popular choice, but there are other options like OpenStreetMap (via plugins).

Using the `google_maps_flutter` Package

To integrate Google Maps in Flutter, add the `google_maps_flutter` package to your `pubspec.yaml`:

```yaml
dependencies:
  flutter:
    sdk: flutter
  google_maps_flutter: ^2.2.1
```

Example of displaying a map:

```dart
import 'package:google_maps_flutter/google_maps_f
```

```
lutter.dart';

GoogleMapController? mapController;

void onMapCreated(GoogleMapController controller) {
  mapController = controller;
}

@override
Widget build(BuildContext context) {
  return GoogleMap(
    onMapCreated: onMapCreated,
    initialCameraPosition: CameraPosition(
      target: LatLng(37.7749, -122.4194),
      zoom: 12.0,
    ),
  );
}
```

Best Practices

- Manage API keys and credentials securely (use environment variables or secure storage).
- Follow platform-specific guidelines for integrating maps, especially for Android and

iOS.

Conclusion

Organizing a Flutter project effectively involves structuring your codebase logically, using appropriate storage solutions for data persistence, and integrating geolocation and maps seamlessly. By following best practices and leveraging Flutter's robust ecosystem of plugins and packages, you can build scalable, maintainable Flutter applications that provide a great user experience. Whether you're developing a simple mobile app or a complex enterprise solution, these principles and techniques will help you deliver high-quality Flutter applications efficiently.

Index

1. Introduction to Flutter pg.4

2. Flutter Installation Guide pg.7

3. Setting Up the Development Environment pg.13

4. Flutter Development: Comprehensive Guide pg.32

5. Fundamentals of Dart (in Flutter) pg.54

6. Advanced Flutter: Building Complex UI and Managing State pg.65

7. Creating a Flutter Application pg.84

8. Advanced Flutter Development: Data Passing, Routing, and State Management pg.98

9. Navigating Between Screens in a Flutter App pg.133

10. Project Organization in Flutter pg.142

www.ingramcontent.com/pod-product-compliance
Lightning Source LLC
Chambersburg PA
CBHW071923210526
45479CB00002B/537